Diary *of a* Pilgrim

Diary of a Pilgrim

Jaydeepsinh G. Vaghela

PARTRIDGE

A Penguin Random House Company

ISBN: Hardcover   978-1-4828-3497-0
               Softcover   978-1-4828-3496-3
               eBook   978-1-4828-3495-6

To order additional copies of this book, contact
Partridge India
000 800 10062 62
orders.india@partridgepublishing.com

www.partridgepublishing.com/india

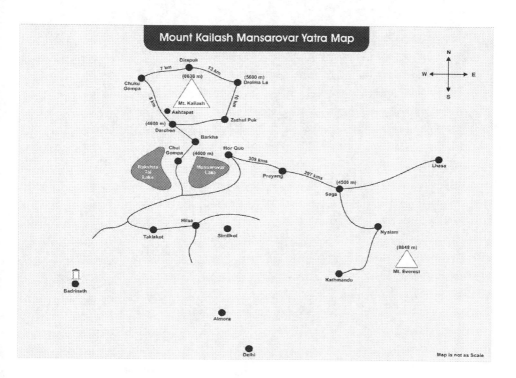

Mount Kailash Mansarovar Yatra Map

1

ON A JOURNEY TO DISCOVER DIVINITY

Date 28th May 2013

Bhagwan Shivji is the God of dispassion, contentment, health and joy. He is the God of the cycle of birth and death. He imparts the divine, esoteric, 'sanatan', and ancient knowledge, which enables an earnest seeker to understand the transient, panoramic world of the duality of sorrow and pleasure, and thereby to become immortal and free from conditioned living and the cycle of reincarnation.

The theory of reincarnation is at the core of religion. As per Gautam Buddha, one life lived for 80 years is a fraction of a second in context of the time of the universe. Each soul lives through billions of lives. In the Bhagawat Gita, Shri Krishna tells the grieving warrior Arjuna that "there was never a time when both, you and I were not there. But you do not remember your past births, whereas I do." He explains the futility of lamenting over the dead as it is impossible to be killed or to kill:

"Thou hast mourned those who should not be
mourned ……..
Nor at any moment was I not,
Nor thou, nor these kings,
And not at all shall we ever come not to be ….."

The region of Kailash- Mansarovar is the abode of Bhahwan Shivji. Many great saints such as Buddah, Rishabhdev, Mahavir, Pandav king Yudhishthir, are believed to have stayed at Mansarovar to meditate and dispel ignorance with divine knowledge. A renowned saint, Shri Swaminarayan, went on a pilgrimage to Kailash, in the 18th century from Badrinath, when he was only 11 years old. An account of his journey is given at www.baps.org. in. Mount Kailash is the symbol of faith and divinity for the four major religions of the world--Hinduism, Jainish, Buddhism and Bompo(religion practiced in Tibet). As per the Hindus and the Buddhists, Kailash is the center of the universe. For the followers of Jain religion Mount Astapada, which is adjoining Kailash, is the place where the first Jain Tirthankar Rishabdev attained Moksha. The followers of Bompo religion, practiced mainly by Tibetans, believe that Kailash is the nine faced mountain which is the controller of all worldly activities. The followers of this religion do the parikrama(circumambulation) of Kailash in the anti-clock wise direction. It is believed that the spiritual energy called 'Prana" by the Hindus and 'Chi' by the Buddhists is the maximum in this region surrounding Kailash. The spiritual energy holds the secret to super-consciousness. In today's age, an educated person with a scientific temper will find many beliefs encoded in ancient scriptures as unscientific and superstitious. But in recent years there are many developments which give credence to mythology. With the advent of modern science, many ancient belief and postulates found in ancient texts are being empirically established. Since the Vedic age, Hindus have believed in the nine planets and their influence on human life. Modern science discovered the planets in our solar system only in the 19th Century. The principles enshrined in the ancient texts reveal many secrets to the wise. Albert Einstein is recorded to have said that he discovered the genesis of his theory of relativity, from the ancient Hindu texts.

The region known as Kailash-Mansarovar is situated in Tibet, which is at present under Chinese occupation. The Mansarovar Lake, which is situated at a height of 14,500 /- feet above sea level, is a freshwater lake at the highest altitude on Earth. The altitude of the region surrounding Mount Kailash where a pilgrim does the 'parikrama' (Circumambulate) of Kailash varies from 1400 to 18,600 feet. The rivers Brahmaputra, Indus, Sutlej, and Karnali–a tributary of Ganga– have their origin in this region. This is the land of miraculous panacea herbs and the immortal and the mystical beings.

Mr. Nensingh Rawat, a surveyor working for the British, was the first person to survey Tibet and measure the height of mountains including the Mount Everest, during the 19th Century. A book titled –'On the back of Tibet' written by Mr. Nensingh Rawat gives an interesting account of the geography of Tibet.

The Tibetan literature on medicine and meditation is acclaimed as unique and valuable.

From India, there are two main routes used by Pilgrims to reach Kailash-Mansarovar. One is via Almora in Uttaranchal by crossing the border at the Lipu Lekh Pass and the second is via Kathmandu in Nepal. Kathmandu is well connected by air and after reaching Kathmandu, one travel's by road to reach Mansarovar. Some also fly to Lhasa in Tibet and then reach Kailash- Mansarovar by road. There is an ancient path-way from the town of Badrinath going to Kailash, which was frequently used mainly by saints during ancient times for reaching Kailash from Badrinath. Before the Chinese occupied Tibet in 1950, this path way was the favorite of the Indian pilgrims going to Kailash. Among these various routes used by Pilgrims, the route via Almora and Lipu Lekh pass is the safest as there are no motorable roads or flights on this route and pilgrims ascend the high altitude slowly while trekking and acclimatizing to the changing higher altitude. The Government of India organizes tours on this route and pilgrims are selected on the basis of a draw or lottery system as there is high demand for this tour package. Pilgrims have to go through a thorough medical check-up, first at Delhi and then at a higher altitude in Uttaranchal. Pilgrims, who fail the test, are deported back. Pilgrims who go directly to Lhasa by flight from Khatmandu and then to Kailash and Mansarovar, are at the greatest risk of being afflicted by mountain sickness as they ascend a height to 8000/- feet within an hour.

For the last one year I had a desire to go to a place which has spiritual and cultural significance and where one can be close to nature and indulge in trekking and adventure sport activities. Since childhood I had heard of Kailash Mansarovar as the holiest of the holy places where God resides. I have deep reverence for Shivji and therefore I decided to go on a pilgrimage to Kailash-Mansarovar. Last year one Parsi friend by the name of Tantum Nanavaty, who was an advocate practicing in the Gujarat High Court had gone on a pilgrimage to Kailash. But he died, before reaching Mansarovar, at a place about 60 kms away from Mansarovar. He was about 50 years of age and was otherwise in good health. This made me cautious and curious and I decided to go fully aware of the hardships one can face at high altitude and in cold climate. I read a lot on the internet and also talked to people who had previously visited Kailash-Mansarovar. One reason for writing this diary is that it can serve as a guide for future pilgrims.

An altitude above 8,000/- feet is considered high altitude. At high altitude, the percentage of oxygen in the air is less, the atmospheric pressure is less and the temperature remains low. This can cause a disease know as mountain sickness. In its mild form, mountain sickness has symptoms such as mild headache, breathlessness and vomiting. In its acute form mountain sickness causes water to accumulate in the lungs and brain. Mountain sickness in its acute form can be life threatening. If not treated in time mountain sickness can result into more serious ailments such as pulmonary edema and cerebral edema. Mountain sickness can be easily prevented by taking some basic precautions. First, before going on pilgrimage, get yourself examined by a doctor. If one is suffering from serious cardiovascular ailments, it is advisable not to go to places higher than 8,000/- feet. If one is suffering from mild diabetes or blood pressure or heart or lung ailments which are not life threatening, one can go. But, in that case, make sure that the tour organizer has a good reputation and is well equipped with doctors and equipments such as oxygen cylinders and has the necessary arrangements to immediately evacuate an ailing pilgrim to lower altitude in case of an emergency. Second, even if you are in good health, you should build up your stamina by regular exercise, especially if you intend to do the 'parikrama'(circumambulation) of Kailash. There is also an age limit imposed by the Government and only those between the ages of 18 to 65 years are eligible for visa to go to Kailash. It is believed that to complete the circumambulation of Kailash, which means trekking at an altitude of 18,600/- feet, faith in Shivji and will power are more potent than lung power or muscular strength. It is said in the Mahabharata that out of the five Pandavs and Draupadi, it was only Yudhisthir who could climb the stairs to Kailash. Arjuna and Bhim, although physically stronger could not do so as they were not as righteous as Yudhisthir. But Faith by itself is not sufficient for a seeker to reach self realization. Faith should be accompanied by efforts and wisdom. It is said that faith and wisdom or discretion are the two tools by which a person can climb the spiritual ladder to reach God. Right action and right attitude are part of the eight fold path given by Buddha for spiritual enlightenment. Therefore, along with faith one should act rationally and be well prepared to undertake the yatra(pilgrimage). While trekking at high altitude, the best precaution against mountain sickness is to ascend slowly-not more than 1,500/- feet in one day. This helps the body to acclimatize to the changing levels of oxygen. Another common ailment at high altitude is dehydration. Ascending slowly, preventing exhaustion, remaining warm, drinking lots of water, smelling Camphor are the cardinal rules to remain fit at high altitude.

There are many tour operators who organize tours to Kailash Mansarovar. But some are novices and can put you through great hardship. Take due care and diligence in selecting the tour operator, especially if you are aged or not in good health. The tour operator essentially does the following: (a) gets a visa for you from the Chinese authorities (b) gets an insurance cover for you (c) arranges for your stay in hotels/dharamshalas during the pilgrimage-tour (d) provides food, assistants, transport etc. during the pilgrimage-tour. I decided to go with a Rajkot based trust by the name of Shiv Vandana Trust run by Professor Yogeshbhai. Before going I asked many of my friends and relatives if they would like to accompany me. But only one- Bhupatsinh Vaghela, who is a distant cousin, agreed to accompany me. Shiv Vandana trust has a tie up with Shresta Tours and Travels in Nepal. From Nepal onwards, the logistics-which includes Sherpas (men), Land Cruiser Cars, buses, food, etc.--is provided by Shresta Tour and Travels. We paid Rs. 1,30,000/- each towards fees for the yatra(pilgrimage), which includes air–fare, hotel stay, meals and insurance. But this does not include expenses which may be incurred for evacuation to a lower altitude in case of an emergency.

After packing the luggage I was left with two bags. One hand bag, weighing about 3 kgs, which I could carry with me on plane and one big bag weighing 18 Kgs., which would go with the luggage in the plane. We boarded an Indigo plane from Ahmedabad at 6.20 a.m, which reached New Delhi at 7.30 a.m. From Delhi we had to catch the flight to Khatmandu in Nepal. For doing so we had to shift our luggage to the international airport from the domestic airport. Although bus service is good, moving with two bags, one of which weighs 18 kgs. is quite a task. We reached Khatmandu in the evening and were transported by bus to a 5 star resort called Gokarna Forest Resort. Ambience in the resort is good, but the food, though offering much variety, did not taste like home food. From today onwards I have made it a routine to write a diary before going to bed, about the information and experiences I collect during the day with a view that my diary may come handy to the pilgrims who undertake the yatra(pilgrimage) in the future

2

KHATMANDU, TOTAPURI AND THE HOT WATER SPRING

Date 29th May, 2013

I woke up in time, took a bath and did puja(prayer). 'Puja' is necessary as it reminds us that we are not on a merry making tour, but on a 'yatra' (pilgrimage). The idea is to exercise restrain and to refrain from indulgence in sense enjoyment, thereby enabling oneself to experience peace and clarity of mind. As per the Hindu Scriptures, the fundamental components of the human body are: (a)the five sense organs- skin(touch), eyes (sight), nose (smell), ears (hearing) and tongue(taste). (b) the five organs of action —two legs, two arms, sex organ, throat (voice) and the excretory organ. (c) 'Antahakaran' consisting of the 'mann'(mind), 'buddhi'(intellect), 'chit'(consciousness) and ego(memory & identification with the body and mind). These components work in perfect unison and coordination to form the organic whole. Information about an external object is received by the sense-organ(s) and it is sent to the mann(mind). Depending on the memory and past experiences, the mann(mind) gives the various options and perceptions for interpreting the object to the Buddhi(intellect). The Buddhi(intellect) then decides as to what is the truth or the correct perception and according to the decision taken by the Buddhi, the organs of action carries out the act. For example, when a man sees a rope on the road, the information of the rope is sent to the mind(mann) by the eyes. The 'mann' then gives the various options accompanied by emotions and feelings such as– it is a snake and the feeling of fear or curiosity, it is a rope which looks like a snake etc. The buddhi then decides which among them the correct perception is. The Buddhi (intellect) is the seat of wisdom. A person is called healthy when all the above components are in good health and are not a source of disturbance to the person.

When on a pilgrimage it is important to eat and sleep moderately and to avoid alcoholic drinks. At high altitude, for a person afflicted with mountain sickness, alcohol is like poison and can cause water to accumulate in the lungs or brain and can cause death within a few hours.

In Nepal there are private planes which fly tourist around Mount Everest and Gauri-Shankar for Rs. 6,500/- per person. Some pilgrims and I bought tickets on a plane called Buddha and saw Everest and Gauri-Shankar from the plane. From above they look like snow-mountains emerging from in-between the snow white clouds. "I have not climbed the Everest, but I have touched it with my heart" read an advertisement to attract tourists. Flying tourist around the Everest appears to be a lucrative business, as there was a long line of tourist waiting to board the plane.

(The mountains Gauri–Shanker and Mount Everest)

The Chinese border is far from Khatmandu, and it takes at least 10 hours to reach the border from Khatmandu. Visa clearance at the border takes many hours and therefore it is advisable to be at the border in the morning, so that visa clearance formalities can be completed in day light, before sunset. Therefore, we left Khatmandu in the afternoon for a place called Totapuri near the border, so that we could start the visa clearance process the next morning. As Totapuri is only 10 kms away from the Chinese border, one can reach China border in the morning and finish the visa clearance by noon and then proceed further in Chinese territory. The way to Totapuri snakes through the hills surrounded by deep valleys and dense forests. The road is quite narrow. On the way to Totapuri, at one place, we had to stop as a boulder had fallen from a mountain and had blocked the road. It was raining heavily and there was a possibility of other loose boulders falling. Therefore, it was necessary for the driver of our bus to take the bus to a safe place. Moreover the sun had set and it was dark. Initially the driver took the bus in reverse gear and after finding a clearance at a curve, he suddenly turned the bus. I was sitting on the last seat in the bus and when the bus turned, I felt as if the bus was hanging over a cliff and was about to fall into the valley. Different persons in the bus reacted differently. Some started shouting at the driver. Some started remembering God. One person by the name of Shamlal started laughing loudly and profusely. May be he found the fear among the other passengers funny.

We were not far from Totapuri and the Sherpas brought a JCB machine from Totapuri and cleared the road. We reached Totapuri at 1 P.m. in the night. Totapuri is at an altitude of about 5,000 feet. The hills surrounding Totapuri are covered with dense forests, deep valleys and high waterfalls. A few yards from the guest house where we were put up, is a hot water spring. For taking a bath in the spring one has to pay a fee of Rs. 10. For a bath in the hot water tub or in a big swimming pool like tub one has to pay Rs. 100/-. It is believed that taking a bath in this holy water cures one of all physical ailments. We paid Rs. 10 each and took a shower under the hot water spring.

People in Nepal speak Hindi and English languages. They have mongoloid features and their political ideology is influenced by the Chinese political ideology, which is communism. But except the mongoloid features they are very much Indian. Their culture is Indian. They are either Hindus or Buddhists. Nepal like India has many temples and monasteries. Perhaps that is why they feel more Indian then Chinese or Tibetan. Nepal is the only Hindu State in the world. Nepal has the rare distinction of being one among the few countries in the world which has remained free from foreign rule and foreign domination. Nepal is the birth place of Gautam Bhuddha and Gorakhnathji. Religion binds people more than political ideologies. Nepalese call the people from Tibet as Bhonte. I talked to some Nepali people in

Totapuri. They are very cultured and courteous. They know about Indian politicians. I was surprised when they said they like Mr. Narendra Modi. They said they watch Indian movies and Indian Television serials. Although the Nepalese look like the Tibetans and the Chinese and are also geographically connected, surprisingly, they cannot converse with people from Tibet or China as their language is different. Totapuri is a small Hill Station located on the bank of river Bhotekoshi. The river is called Bhote as it comes from Tibet. One thing I noted in Nepal rural areas is that houses have door and windows, but windows, even ground floor windows, do not have iron or steel grills, and, have only glass shutters in wooden frames. I' am told thefts are extremely rare in Nepal rural areas.

(Nepali girls at Totapani in Nepal)

3

CROSSING THE FRIENDSHIP BRIDGE

Date 30th May, 2013

Today we had to finish the visa formalities and proceed towards Tibet. The guest house where we were put up is on the bank of river Bhontekoshi, which comes from Tibet. From the dining hall of the guest house we could see a cluster of houses on a very high mountain across the river. We are told that the village on the top of the hill was inhabited by people with their livestock. We reached the China border at about 11 a. m. There is a bridge over the river Bhontekoshi which connects Nepal with China. It is called the friendship bridge. Photography is strictly prohibited in this area. Some pilgrims who were not aware of this were visited by angry Chinese soldiers who snatched away their cameras and said something which we could not understand. But the cameras were returned after some time. I was not aware that photography is banned therefore I took one photograph of a Chinese building on the Chinese side. While I was taking the photograph one Chinese soldier looked at me with an angry soldier like gaze, this made me realize that the soldiers did not like it and therefore I quickly put away the camera in my bag. Maybe he did not come for my camera as when the photograph was clicked I was standing on the other side of the bridge, in Nepal territory.

What was unusual at the Chinese border was that an elderly gentleman, who was perhaps a high ranking Chinese officer, with a constant smile on his face kept watching us-the pilgrims-for about two hours while we were waiting for visa clearance. He was taking our photographs with a camera which had a zoom lens. The zoom lens was about 6 inches long. He took photographs when we were waiting in groups and also photographs of each individual pilgrim when we were returned our passport after being individually examined by a Chinese official.

From China border we were provided with Toyota Land Rovers. We formed groups with four pilgrims in each group. One Land Rover driven by a Chinese driver was given to each group. The four persons in my group were myself, Bhupatsinh, Shamlal and Parmarbhai. The Chinese driver did not understand Hindi or English, but when shown a photograph of Bhagwan Shivji, he smiled and said "Shiva, Shiva." From the border we headed for Nayalam in Land Rovers jeeps. The 80 kms drive from the China border to Nayalam is marked by high mountains, deep valleys and dense forests. The Road is cement road and is broad-about 6 meters- and in very good condition. Once you enter China, you find that the cemented roads are in good condition and kept very clean.

We reached Nayalam in the evening. Nayalam is at about 10,000/- feet above the sea level and is a fairly big Chinese town.

It is biting cold and even the natives have covered themselves with warm clothes and caps. After reaching Nayalam, many pilgrims experienced mild headache. Some even vomited. Symptoms of mountain sickness appear after 6 to 8 hours after going to a higher altitude. We have to stay in Nayalam for at least one full day in order to acclimatize our bodies with the rising altitude. From Nayalam onwards taking Dimox (medicine) twice daily is compulsory.

(The city of Nayalayam in China)

4

ACCLIMATIZING TO THE HIGH ALTITUDE AT THE CITY OF NAYALAM

Date 31st May

Nayalam is a developed Town with hotels and shops and a prominently located Police station. One can purchase warm clothes, caps, shoes and other articles for the journey ahead, from here. I am told this was the last big town on way to Mansarover. Shop keepers charge exorbitantly and food and other things are very expensive. We are given Dimox twice a day after meals. We are told to take long walks in the morning and evening to acclimatize to higher altitude.

The shops and hotels in Nayalam are located on either side of the main road, and are almost touching the road. The room allotted to us is facing the main road and it is shared by four of us. At 3. p.m in the night Shamlal woke me up and said "I can hear sounds of girls giggling and people talking on the road below, let us go downstairs on the road and see what is happening." We went on the road and saw well dressed young people going towards a building opposite the police station. We could hear music coming from the building. It appeared as if there was some late night dance party in the building.

(Tibetan dog called Bhontia in Nayalam)

5

TO PRAYANK AND BEYOND

Date-1st June

We left Nayalam at 8 a.m. for Prayank, which is at an altitude of 13,000 feet. Until Nayalam our route was full of dense forest and flowing streams and deep valleys and high waterfalls. But a few kilometers from Nayalam we reached a plateau where there was not a single tree in sight. The trees and the deep valleys were replaced by open land surrounded with snow covered mountain tops. The sky is deep blue and bright with cool breeze and snow white clouds touching the mountains. I took some photographs, but felt that the camera was not able to capture the beauty of Tibet. Beauty is to be felt and cannot be seen or captured through a camera lens. Besides the pristine natural beauty, Tibet is also the land of the spiritualist, the flying Yogis and the occult, where paranormal activity is studied as a science. The folklore of Tibet is replete with stories of miracles performed by the eighth century Buddhist Monk called Padmasambhava. The story of his life is similar to that of Gautam Bhuddha. He was the son of a king of north India. He renounced worldly life in search of truth.

In Tibet he was trained by the Sky-Dakinis. Sky-Dakinis are the invisible angels of compassion. Padmasambhava traversed the length and breadth of Tibet and converted the kings, war lords, commoners to Buddhism. Attempts to immolate him on a pyre of fire became futile as the fire turned to either water or sesame oil. Padmasambhava is said to have left behind his footprints on stone at various places in Tibet. These footprints housed in Monasteries are worshiped by the Tibetan monks. At the end of his life he went inside a cave with a disciple and meditated. It is said that after remaining in a trance for seven days his body was converted to 'rainbow body' leaving behind only his hair, nails and the disciple. In Tibet stories of saints converting their body into light form is not uncommon. A 20th century saint, Swami Rama who founded the Himalayan Institute of Yoga is said to have met a yogi in Tibet who converted his body into light form and vanished in thin air. All that is born has to wither and die one day-this appears to be the universal truth. But theoretically if matter is put in a very high state of vibration it converts into light. The smallest unit of matter called the atom- consisting of electrons, protons and space- is nothing but energy or light. For some yogis, converting the body into light form is the ultimate aim of life. Swami Padmasambhava is said to have left behind a treasure trove of literature on Vedic science and spiritualism. But most of it was destroyed due to the negligence of the monks and the invasion on Tibet by the British and the Chinese forces. Among the many books on spiritualism found in the Monasteries, one book know by the westerners' as 'The Tibetan Book Of The Dead' and by the Tibetans as 'Liberation by Hearing' is widely circulated and is very popular among the travelers. As per this book, said to have been penned by Swami Padmasambhava, after a person dies he does not leave the mundane world for about 42 days. He can see and hear his kith and kin mourning over his death, but he cannot communicate with them. Thereafter, he sees a white moon like light emanating peace and tranquility. A trained yogi is attracted by the calmness and joy emanating from the light and he immediately tunes in with the frequency of the light, hears celestial music, gets absorbed in the light and attains Moksha. But an ordinary man is not inclined to let go the illusory world. He then hears a voice which says "O Child of Buddha-nature, that which is called death has now arrived. You are leaving this world. But in this you are not alone. This happens to everyone…….." If these first invocations fail the soul is further pushed into delusion and depending upon the deeds of the past life, the soul sees demons and ghost stamping over it and drawing and drinking blood from its brain. At this stage if the soul can overcome the demons by recognizing its true nature and seeing the demons as emanations of the self, then the soul moves into the realm of Bodhisattva. The dead then hear a voice which says "O Child of Buddha-Nature, where such visions arise, do not be afraid or terrified. Your body is a mental body, formed by habitual tendencies. Therefore, even if you are slain or cut in pieces, you will not die." If the soul cannot overcome the delusions, then it becomes more wretched. The soul in its astral body can move anywhere at will. It floats over its old home, but cannot communicate with its loved ones. It's suffering increases. It is haunted by its past actions and the demons become more terrifying. If the soul has guilt consciousness of having committed a murder, then the undying spirit is beheaded and dismembered again and again. Even after this if the soul does not recognize the sufferings as illusory and cannot detach itself, the soul is then condemned to reincarnation. There are prayers and rituals which enables the dead to be reborn in a particular womb. Interesting account of the Kailash Mansarovar region is also given in a book penned by the 20th century saint Swami Bhagwan Hamsa. In his book he has described his miraculous escape from a python, lusting wild elephant and licentious mountain woman. While circling Kailash, he was caught in a hail storm, but with Sivji's grace he survived. In the olden days Hindu saints use to undertake a journey to Kailash from the pilgrimage place of Badrinath in India. This route from Badrinath to Kailash is perhaps the shortest one from India.

(A Tibetan village)

On way to Prayank we stopped at a place called Sangha for lunch. Sangha appears to be an old town and most of its inhabitants on the outskirts near the highway are Tibetans. I saw a young Tibetan seated in a shop adjacent to the road where we had parked our cars. I approached the Tibetan and tried to converse with him. But we did not understand each other's language and except the smiles which conveyed that he was pleased to see me, there was nothing I could understand from the signs he made with his hands and the words he spoke. Out of the various sounds he was making one sound sounded like lama. This reminded me of Dalia Lama and so I said 'Dalai Lama' and 'Dharamshala'. This pleased him greatly and there was an instant reaction from him and he asked me to come inside the shop and offered me a chair. He brought a silk shawl from one of the cupboards and put it across my shoulders. He wanted to honor me. I gave him a small packet of dry fruits.

In the early 20th century, certain areas of Tibet were under Chinese government. But after the Communist Party of China came to power, these areas were liberated and it is said that the Chinese had even apologized to the then Dalai Lama. But in 1950, the Chinese army invaded and occupied Tibet and in the process killed lacks of Buddhists and destroyed thousands of monasteries. The armies of Dalai Lama were no match for the mechanized army of China. The Dalai Lama and many of his disciples fled to India and established themselves at Dharamshala in Himachal Pradesh. There is one monastery near Lasha, where the statue of Buddha has tears in its eyes. It is said that when the Chinese came to destroy the statue, a miracle happened and the statue started shedding tears. This softened the Chinese and they left the statue unharmed. Ironically, the Chinese call this invasion of Tibet as the Cultural Revolution. Perhaps the Buddhist culture was replaced by the Chinese culture. Even today worshiping Dalai Lama is a punishable offence in Tibet. Notwithstanding the Chinese efforts to forever erase the traces of Dalai Lama from Tibet, even after 50 years Dalai Lama is very much alive in the hearts of the Tibetans-even young Tibetans. A faint call from him can push Tibet into an era of insurgencies and war. But fortunately, Dalai Lama is a true Buddhist and despite the violence perpetuated by the Chinese, he remains non-violent and does not advocate violent methods to liberate Tibet. China is an ancient civilization like India and Chinese people of today have many qualities like honesty, cleanliness, sincerity, discipline, which Lord Buddha preached, but sadly they are lacking in compassion. Chinese have brought modern education to Tibet and have also improved the standard of nourishment by making various grains and pulses grown in mainland China available to the Tibetans. The Chinese unified Tibet and introduced modern medical and educational services and developed the infrastructure-roads, telecommunication, hotels, hospitals etc. in Tibet.

China has only one political party which is the Communist Party of China. China is a republic but it cannot be called a democracy. Chinese do not believe in protecting individual freedom and freedom is sacrificed for what is perceived as the greater common good. The local people we saw along the road looked poor and filthy and were dressed in old dirty clothes with unkempt beards and hair. But the Chinese Police men are young and smart and neatly dressed and looked very fit. However they were not carrying guns. The well maintained, clean public places and roads and the Chinese Police gives an impression that the Government is working. It seems that the Chinese believe in hard work and orderliness. China is a world power and is known for using military might, in complete disregard of The United Nations Organization, for settling disputes with its neighboring countries. Considering the rising economic and military might of China, some people in India are of the opinion that the

Countries on the international borders of China should unite and form an association or enter into a treaty to help each other in the event of a Chinese aggression or invasion on anyone of them.

We reached Prayank in the late evening. Prayank is a small village. As it was 10.30 p.m. and the sun had set, we had to break journey and spend the night at Prayank, which is at a distance of 60 kms. from Mansarovar lake. We stayed at a guest house located on the highway. At the entrance of the guest house there is a board of India Heritage Foundation, which is an NGO based in India. I'am told that the guest house was constructed by India Heritage Foundation for pilgrims going to Mansarovar. The guesthouse has single storey small rooms arranged in a square, so that when the gate is closed the area becomes a closed enclosure. The quality of material used in the rooms is good, but there are no bathrooms. One has to go in the open to answer the call of nature. From Nayalam onwards it is so cold that one even goes to bed with the warm clothes one is wearing during the day. Taking a bath seems impossible.

After dinner, when we were in our rooms, I counted my pulse rate as I wanted to know how my heart was coping with the changing altitude. I found that my pulse rate was 130 beats per minute. I knew that normally the heart beats at 70 beats per minute. This made me very anxious and I was suddenly gripped with the fear that my heart was malfunctioning and that it may cause other complications. My other roommates in the room had gone to sleep and I did not want to wake them up. Therefore, I tried to meditate and practice 'Savasan'(dead pose) to bring down the pulse rate. But it did not work and the more I tried to calm myself the more and more anxious I became. I could not sleep. I became so conscious of the pulse rate that I could hear my heart pulsating. I could not sleep for the whole night as all my attention was on bringing down the pulse rate. Early morning the next day, I woke up Bhupatsingh and told him that my pulse rate was very high. But he being a villager did not understand and said "what is that?" Ignorance is bliss. I measured his pulse rate and to my great surprise found that his heart was also beating at 135 beats per minute. I told him that the pulse rate should be 72 per minute and if it beats too fast it may stop working. He also looked worried. We went to the doctor and complained that we had been inflicted by some disease as our hearts were beating too fast. The doctor had a small instrument which was put on my finger. The instrument showed the oxygen level as 8 and pulse rate as 130 per minute. After reading the instrument the doctor said "you are in very good condition and your heart is doing fine." I could not understand and said "sir can you please explain why our hearts are beating at 135 beats per minute instead of 72". The doctor started laughing and explained that even his heart was beating at 130 beats per minute. At high altitude the heart rate of a healthy human heart ranges from 120 to 140 beats per minute. Heart rate of less than 120 at that altitude is abnormal and can be fatal. One other person by the name of Parmarbhai, who was also in my room, had a pulse rate of 90 per minute. He was given some medication and was told not to do the Parikrama(circumambulation) of Kailash.

6

THE SACRED MANSAROVAR LAKE

Date 2ⁿᵈ June

We left Prayank early morning before sun rise for the Mansarovar lake. We had seen many photographs of the Mansarovar lake on the internet and in books and each one of us had his own individual fantasy of what the Mansarovar lake would be like. The thought that we were going to actually take a bath in the holiest of the holy Mansarovar lake and spend the next few days in the Kailash-Mansarovar region, really excited us.

We reached Mansarovar lake at 11 a.m. From a distance the Mansarovar lake looks like a vast sea of deep blue water being nourished by the golden rays of the sun and the pure cool breeze. The shores of the Mansarovar lake has sand and one feels as if one is on a sea beach. About 200 meters away from the Mansarovar lake there are rooms made from metal sheets for the pilgrims. Ten pilgrims are accommodated in one such room. I was expecting to see Buddhist Monasteries around Mansarovar, as in the recorded accounts of saints, posted on web-sites such as www.baps.org.in, there is a mention of two storey monasteries around Mansarovar. One saint who came to Mansarovar before

1950, stayed in one such monastery during the winter. He has described the Mansarovar lake as frozen ice lake reflecting moon light and even more beautiful than in summer. I was disappointed that we were not staying in a Monastery among monks. But the rooms were we are staying have sand on the floor and are quite comfortable. However, there are no bathrooms. Perhaps the Chinese Government has purposely not allowed construction around Mansarovar so as to protect and preserve the natural environment. Allowing large scale construction and investment to make this place a holiday destination for the rich can be disastrous for this region.

The natural environment consists of various intervened eco-systems intricately connected to form an interdependent and coherent whole web. A disturbance in one eco-system gets transmitted to other eco-systems. Trillions of atoms of hydrogen, nitrogen, oxygen and other gases are continuously processed and recycled between the lithosphere, ionosphere and hydrosphere so as to create and maintain a perfect balance which can sustain life. A disturbance in this fine balance invites nature's fury in the form of storms, earthquakes, floods etc. Ecology is a very complex science and scientist have failed to give a satisfactory explanation as to how the environment works and exactly what is it that sustains the environment. The Biodiversity- the various microbes, plant and animals- found in a certain region creates and maintains the environment of that region. Even if one species of a certain microbe found in a certain region were to become extinct, the functioning of the environment of that region will be adversely affected. Rivers are known to dry up if a certain species of fish found in the river becomes extinct. In India one can notice the change in the natural environment after every few hundred kilometers. Certain species of plants and animals found in one region will not be found in another region just 100 kilometers away. The region of Kailash-Mansarovar has its own unique environment. There is not a single tree in this region. Mosquitoes and other insects commonly found in the plains do not exist here. The Mansarovar lake has its own unique eco-system. The area immediately surrounding the lake is full of sand and small stone-pebbles of different colors and shapes. The shrubs found in the plains surrounding Mansarovar are said to have many potent medicinal properties. The Tibetans believe that these miraculous shrubs can cure any disease. According to the local Tibetans and the Sherpas there are no reptiles in the lake. There are no swans or ducks in the lake, but a species of fat, rounded birds with white and grey feathers and a sharp beak are in plenty around Mansarovar lake. The pristine beauty of the Mansarovar lake appears intact and untouched by the pollution caused by development in other parts of the world. The possibility of this region becoming a major tourist hot spot is scarce because of the harsh and unpredictable weather conditions, low atmospheric pressure and low level of oxygen in the air. This region remains covered with snow for most part of the year. Notwithstanding the incessant developmental activities in other parts of the world, Kailash Mansarovar will perhaps always retain its natural beauty and ecological balance and will always remain a revered place for the times to come.

We were told that Kailash was on our right side, when facing Mansarover. But it was cloudy and we could not have darshan of Kailash. It was biting cold and windy, and the temperature was below 5 degree centigrade. We are told that normally it is not so cold, but the previous day the weather had changed and the batch of pilgrims who came before us were not allowed to go on parikrama(circumambulation) of Kailash as there was heavy snow fall in the Kailash region. Mansarovar lake has surface area of about 300 kms. and its depth at certain places is about 180 meters. Its circumference measures 80 kms.

(The Mansarovar lake)

We were looking forward to having a bath in the Mansarvor. But now that we were standing in the Mansarovar, we found it difficult to gather enough courage to even take off our warm clothes and take a dip in its ice cold water. Some people take the Mansarovar water to the kitchen and heat it and thereafter bathe with it. After some warming up exercise, I took off my clothes and walked into the Mansarovar till I reached knee deep water. I soaked the 'Rudraks-mala'(rosary of Rudraks beads), which I had bought in Nepal, in the water as it is believed that soaking the mala in water and praying to Shivji makes the 'mala' fit for japa(repetition of God's name). Thereafter I sat on my knees and soaked my head and body in the water. I started shivering and my arms and hands started shaking violently. I immediately got up on my feet and despite taking deep breaths and tightening the body I could not control my shaking hands. I was afraid that I may lose the rudraks mala and I squeezed it firmly in my fist. But then I looked up at the sun, which was brightly shining in the sky. Suddenly I felt some warmth. I kept gazing at the sun for some time. I again took one dip in the water and then got up and gazed for some time at the sun. In this manner I took six dips. Most others, who failed to notice the sun, could manage only one dip. It is believed that by taking a bath in the lake, one becomes free from the karmic debts.

After the bath in the lake we gathered in small groups and performed 'havan', and, Dr. Yogeshbhai, who is a Brahmin and well versed in Vedic hums recited the mantras. I have performed the ceremony of 'havan'(a form of prayer by lighting a fire and reciting mantras and making offerings of wood and certain herbs in the fire) many times in the past. But today it was different. The slanting golden rays of the sun piercing the clean cool air and lighting the environment, coupled with the feeling of purity and lightness as if all the dirt, negativity and heaviness was washed away from me by the bath in the Mansarovar lake, made me feel completely quiet, peaceful and connected to the joy or anand of Shiva. My whole being got filled with love, complete surrender and devotion to Shiva. A Vedic chant describes the cosmic power of Shiva.

> There is nothing apart from Shiva,
> There is nothing other than Shiva,
> Whatever there is, is Shiva,
> There is nothing that is not Shiva,
> There is no time that is not Shiva,
> There is no place that is not Shiva,
> Remembering the all-pervasive consciousness
> Seated in the heart, we bow to Lord Shiva.

There was a Tibetan boy who was constantly in look out for plastic bags, cans, bottles, paper etc. left behind by the pilgrims at the Mansarovar. He would immediately come and pick up the waste material, even before the pilgrims could do so. In return he did not beg or ask for rewards. I could not talk to him as he did not understand my language, but from his demeanor it appeared that he was providing free service. There is a tradition of giving 'dan' or donation after performing 'havan'. Accordingly, after the 'havan' we gave some yens (Chinese currency) to this boy. The credit for keeping the shores of Mansarover clean goes to this boy.

After the Havan, we had lunch and retired to our rooms. At high altitude one looses interest in food. Eating one chapatti and some dry fruits fill the stomach. I developed a dislike for food such as chpattis and dry fruits. However, I enjoyed eating spicy food such as 'chevdas', eaten more in Gujarat. There is a liquid energy drink called Red Bull available at Mansarovar. Having one such bottle gives enough energy for day to day activity. Perhaps energy requirement of the body decreases at higher altitude. However, at high altitude it is believed that one should eat food rich in carbohydrates such as raisins, chocolates and dry fruits in order to remain physically fit. At Mansarovar the sun sets at 10.30 p.m. There is hardly any difference between sun rise and sun set. Both appear almost the same. We took a walk by the lake side until late in the evening. At 10 p.m. one can see the sun setting and the sky gradually becoming dark. Sun rise is at 6.30 a.m.

(Tibetan goat near Mansarovar lake)

7

THE RAKSHAH-THAL LAKE AND THE CITY OF DARCHEN

Date 3rd June

Today at about 3.30 a.m., I had a dream that a saint was walking in the dark by the side of Mansarovar lake. The saint had a jata – hair knots tied by rudraks beads– on his head which was about one feet in height. As it was dark, I could not see the face or other features, except that he had broad shoulders. But strangely, even in the dream, I could feel that the saint was deeply calm, strong and determined with a thoughtless or one pointed mind not disturbed by thoughts. After the dream I woke up and saw the watch. It was 3.30 a.m. It was only after I woke up that I realized that Shivji, in his photographs that we find in temples and elsewhere, has a big 'jata' tied by rudrakhs beads. The saint in my dream could be Shivji. I was feeling completely refreshed and my lungs felt as if they were full of oxygen. Being refreshed and joyful, I immediately took the rudrakhs 'mala' and went to the shore of Mansarovar. Shamlal was also awake and he accompanied me. We sat on the shore till 5 a.m and I did 11 rounds of the mala of Shiv mantra. I had heard stories of pilgrims seeing lights coming from the sky at dawn and taking a dip in the water or just giving darshan to the pilgrims. However we did not see any lights coming from the sky.

As per our schedule 4th 5th and 6th June are fixed for parikrama (circumambulation) of Mount Kailash. Our parikrama is to start on the 4th morning from a place called Yam Dwar which is near a town called Darchen. As per the Hindu traditions, circumambulation or 'parikrama' of a holy place has great spiritual significance, as it is believed that circumambulation of a holy place washes away ones sins committed in the past. Today that is on the 3rd we are to reach Darchen and also complete half the parikrama of Mansarovar by road. The remaining half will be completed on our way back from Kailash. We left Mansarovar at 8 a.m for Darchen by bus. The weather had improved and unlike yesterday today it was bright, sunny and very pleasant. The temperature inside the bus was 8 degree centigrade and it was not windy today.

(The Lake Mansarovar)

We stopped at a place which is narrow stretch of land between the Mansarovar lake and another lake called Rakshastal. To the north of Rakshahthal is the Magnificent Kailash. It appears like a majestic lone mountain covered with snow. The first glimpse of Kailash reminded me of the Taj Mahal at Agra. But I found Kailash more enchanting, pure, holy and grand then the Taj Mahal first seen after entering the gate of the Taj Complex. Although both lakes are adjacent to each other with a narrow strip of land separating the two, the lake Rakshasthal is a contrast of Mansarovar. Mansarover has birds and other life forms living in it or near it, but Rakshastal, although adjoining Mansarovar, does not have any life forms. Birds and other creature do not go near the Rakshastal. Also, it is windier on the shores of Rakshahtal. Perhaps it is a salt water lake. There is a small island at the center of Rakshastal. It is said that the demon king Ravana sat on this island for a 1000 years and worshiped Shivji. Shivji being pleased by Ravana's devotion asked Ravan to ask for a boon. Ravana had the desire to rule the world and therefore he prayed that he be granted a boon so that neither the devtas nor the rakshas can defeat or slay him. His wish was granted. But Ravana considered humans too weak and inferior and in his arrogance he forgot humans while asking for the boon. Lord Rama in human form defeated Ravana. After we were told the story of Ravana and Rakshastal, we were in agreement that we are also in part Ravana and in part Rama. When we become desperate for money and power we slog it out for a 1000 years like Ravana and become sick and stressed out and end up like Ravana and when we are seeking peace of mind, knowledge of the self and who we really are, we are creative, we evolve, improve and become like Rama.

(The lake Rakshastal)

We reached Darchen in the afternoon at about 3 a.m. Darchen is a big Chinese town and we found that a lot of construction activity was going on in Darchen. There is a telephone booth from where most of us made telephone calls to our family in India. But Shamlal again behaved differently. He said he had told his family to forget him for the fifteen days that he was on pilgrimage. His argument is that true pilgrimage and devotion is possible only if one becomes detached from the worldly affairs and forgets one's family, friends and enemies. I agree with him. The hotel in Darchen where we are staying is like a modern hotel found in big cities, but unfortunately here also there are no bathrooms or toilets. Just outside the hotel there is a large size shop selling handicrafts goods made by the local Tibetan people. We are told that the people of Darchen had constructed a tall statue of Swami Padamasambhava on the outskirts of Darchen, but the Chinese army put a rope around its neck and pulled it down. Installing statues in public places is a trend which has started only in the 20th century. In Hindu and Buddhist cultures, people did not believe in immortalizing their kings and saints by installing their statues in public places. Statutes were made only of Gods and Temples were perhaps the only places were statues were enshrined.

(The city of Darchen)

From the window of our room in Darchen, we could have 'darshan' of Mount Kailash. Mount Kailash is conical in shape with slant pyramidal sides. It does not form a part of the Himalayan ranges. It is isolated from the Himalayas and stands majestically on a flat plateau at about 16,500/- feet, surrounded by the plains and lakes of Tibet. The summit of Kailash at 22,000/- feet has never been scaled. In the year 1715 a Jesuit missionary Ippolito Desideri while travelling from Kashmir to Lasha came across Kailash and had this to say about Kailash "a mountain of excessive height and great circumference, always enveloped in clouds covered in snow and ice, and most horrible, barren, steep and cold.......... The Tibetans walk devoutly round the base of the mountain, which takes several days, and they believe this will bring them great indulgences. Owing to the snow on this mountain, my eyes became so inflamed that I well nigh lost my sight." He was the first European in recorded history to have set his sight on Kailash. But being preoccupied and obsessed with the external form, perhaps he failed to experience the spiritual energy and mysticism surrounding Kailash. Barring a few exceptions, both the believers and non-believers who visited Kailash were invariably touched and moved by the divinity of Kailash. During the summer season the snow on the south face of Kailash melts exposing the scarps on the almost vertical ascent, creating an illusion of a stair case leading to the summit of Kailash. Even during summers, the south face remains almost completely covered with snow from the bottom to the top of Kailash.

There is no recorded account of any person having reached the summit of Kailash. In the ancient Hindu epic Ramayana, written by the sage Valamiki, there is mention of Shri Ramchandra reaching heaven by climbing the stairs of Kailash. In 1926, Colonel Wilson of the Indian Army attempted to scale Kailash. After surveying the southern face with the help of local Tibetans, he identified a ridge which he thought would lead him to the summit. But being faced with the almost vertical ascent and unpredictable and freakish storms of snow and lightening they were disheartened and were left with no option but to retreat. In the past, many great Mountaineers made plans to scale Kailash, but such plans were repeatedly abandoned at their inception due to lack of interest and difficulty in finding local guides or because they were denied permission by the Chinese Government.

The Tibetans believe that there is an invisible ladder from Kailash which goes to heaven. The great kings of ancient Tibet are believed to have descended on Kailash from heaven with their heads attached to ropes of light. The belief that such ropes of light can take a worthy mortal to heaven from Kailash is common among the Tibetans. Tibetans have deep faith in Kailash as the abode of their Gods, and will not tolerate any attempt to disturb its pristine glory with modern machines and mountaineering expeditions. The axus-mundi-the center of the Hindu Buddhist Cosmos is at Kailash. With Kailash as the center point, the universe unfolds as the petals of a lotus. Kailash know by the Hindus as Meru Parvat pervades the ancient Hindu texts. The Hindu temples are built in a conical shape resembling Kailash, as they too are the abode of the Gods.

(Mount Kailash)

8

THE FIRST DAY OF THE CIRCUMAMBULATION (PARIKRAMA) OF KAILASH

Date 4th June

Our parikrama(circumambulation) of Kailash starts from a place called Yam- Dwar, which is a few kilometers away from Darchen. The Parikrama route is Yam Dwar to Drira Phuk to Drolma Pass to Zutrul Phuk to Darchen. Yam-dwar(the gate of Lord Yama) is a small gate constructed of stone. It is believed that on passing through the gate of Yam Dwar, a pilgrim is freed from the fear of death. Pilgrims put photographs of their parents and relatives, who have passed away in front of the Yam Dwar, as it is believed that by putting the photographs and praying at Yam Dwar one can give the 'punya'-merit earned by undertaking the padyatra(circumambulation on foot) or parikrama to the departed soul and thereby help the departed soul to attain salvation. Pilgrimage is also a good 'Karma' like charity or truthfulness or selfless service. It adds to ones spiritual merit. I had brought a photograph of my mother and I placed the photograph on a platform on the wall of the Yam Dwar. I was suddenly overcome by emotions of love and grief and I felt my throat choking. With some conscious effort and by fixing my mind in the present, I shrugged off the debilitating emotions and prayed that the merit if any earned by me by this 'patyatra'(circumambulation on foot) may be passed on to my mother. Emotions tend to possess those who get carried away by them. To be carried away by emotions is bondage. To be a silent witness to them as they wane and die is freedom. From Yam Dwar, a pilgrim can do the parikrama either on horse- back or on foot. The charge per horse is around Rs.25,000. One can hire a horse en-route from a place other than Yam Dwar, but in that case the charge is Rs. 1,000/- per kilometer. If you want to carry a bag or other baggage on the horse along with you, you have to pay extra. Hiring a horse does not mean that one does not have to walk at all. On the second day of the Parikrama one has to climb the Drolma Pass. One does not require mountaineering equipments to climb the Drolma Pass, but it is relatively steep and because of the high altitude, climbing it is quite strenuous. Pilgrims have to leave the horses at the foot of the Drolma Pass. After crossing the Drolma Pass, one can again resume the parikrama on horse-back for the rest of the Parikrama.

(Yam Dwar)

(Tibetan horsemen with Tibetan horses)

From Yam Dwar, Driera phuk is 15 kms away. We had to reach Dera Punkh before sunset. We had sufficient time as we had reached Yam Dwar quite early in the day. Walking 15 kms at an altitude of 17,000 feet is quite different from walking at lower latitudes. After walking a short distance- about 50 meters one fees exhausted. But for those who are in the habit of doing aerobic exercises and are physically fit it is not much of a problem. I and Bhupatsinh took a mala in our hand and kept walking reciting the Shiv mantra. I did not find it strenuous at all. But if one tries to run or walk fast one start panting and heaving for breath. There are streams running down from the Kailash and crossing the path where the pilgrims walk. We were walking by the side of the west face of the Kailash and parallel to the river Lha Chu. On the west face there is a formation of stone and snow which resembles the head of the Shivji's cow- Nandi. The streams emerging from the Kailash and flowing down and across the path-way reminds one of the Shiv Temples where the water comes from the temple and forms a stream outside the temple.

(The west face of Kailash)

We came across a Buddhist lady doing Parikrama (circumambulation) of Kailash. Buddhist call it is as the 'Kora' of Kailash. She was stretching her arms towards the sky and then bringing them in the position of Namaste and then bringing them further down to the knees and then laying down flat on the ground and then moving one foot forward and getting up in the standing position and then repeating the ritual. This way she was to complete the entire parikrama. She appeared to be an educated lady and when I asked her if I may photograph her she smiled and said 'yes you can'. Although her clothes and hair were soiled and dirty, she appeared happy and relaxed. She is to do the entire kora or parikrama (circumambulation) of Kailash, which means covering the distance of 58 Kms through the ups and downs in the hills in this manner. For a young healthy Buddhist it takes a minimum 15 days to complete the Kora. Buddhist repeat the mantra **"Om Mani Padme Hum"** while doing the Kora. It means 'Hail to the Jewel in the Lotus'. The lotus is the body and the Jewel the soul. A pilgrim doing Kora is determined to achieve a consciousness free from sufferings and grief and depression. If one loudly recites the mantra-**"Om Namah Shivay"** and the mantra **"Om Mani Padme Hum"**, one can notice that both mantras are similar and create similar vibrations in the body. Reciting mantras is a form of yoga, which endows the practitioner with peace of mind and good health. Bhagwan Krishna says in the Geeta that "among the yogas, I'am the mantra Yoga". What Buddha called Nirvan is know by the Hindus as Moksha and the Christians know it as self-realization. It is not merely having a positive outlook to life but it is becoming free from the cycle of birth and death and having a consciousness forever drenched in 'ananda'(bliss). One saint once told me that after many hours of meditation, he experiences a kind of bliss rushing forth from within, which cannot be described in words. According to him, although this experience of bliss lasts only for a few seconds, it is a thousand times more pleasurable or enjoyable then a sexual orgasm. A self realized person is believed to be in a continuous state of bliss or super consciousness, unknown to worldly people.

(A Buddhist doing kora of Kailash)

Buddha preached the middle path. Can it be said that doing Kora, done in the aforesaid manner is a middle path to worship. Is it not abusing the body? Looking to the quiet and relaxed demeanor of the lady I have no doubt that she was enjoying the kora and was not abusing her body or mind. In worldly activities there is passion and acquisition. Spiritual pursuits are about giving, experiencing, being and transforming. In worldly pursuits man enjoys the various delicacies and the various sensations of the sense organs and the satisfaction of ego and becomes happy. In spiritual pursuits man enjoys the emptiness and stillness of the mind, lightness and freshness of the body, calmness and purity and becomes joyous and happy. After all life is a pursuit of happiness.

On the way to Drira Phunk, we came across some tents which were supposed to be restaurants run by Tibetan people. One elderly gentleman who was walking with us told us to take some food and refreshments as it was mid-afternoon. We entered one of the tents and sat down on low height wooden benches. The tents were of low height and after sitting on the benches our heads almost touched the tent roof. We asked for a few bottles of the energy drink-Red Bull- and water. After some time a short, fat, middle aged Tibetan woman approached us and started shouting at us and pointed her finger at the outlet of the tent. We could not understand what she was saying. But we could make out from her voice and the expressions on her face that she was angry and wanted us to get out of the tent. My companions felt offended and they refused to get up and they kept sitting with a frown on their faces. I was carrying two small plastic bags containing almonds. Due to the cold climate food items are put into small plastic bags and sealed. For the last few days I had lost all interest in solid food, especially dry fruits and I was thinking of giving away the almonds to Tibetan children. Seeing that the lady was poor and was feeling deprived, I gave her one bag of almonds. She immediately took the bag and gave me a broad smile and walked away. After some time she came back. But this time she was smiling. I gave her the second bag of almonds. She smiled, took the bag and immediately turned around. When it comes to pleasing one's wife, mother or sister, I had always known the power of gifts. But today for the very first time I realized that it also worked on strangers.

It took us 10 hours to walk the distance of 15 kilometers and reach Drira Punkh. Among the pilgrims who were walking with us, I could notice that those who had the will and determination to walk were faring better than those who were fearful and doubtful. One person who had mild diabetes was finding it extremely difficult to walk after we had some snacks and energy drink mid-way. Even while he was having snacks he was having an apprehension that he will not be able to walk after taking snacks as he had diabetes. Walking here is hard work. Persons with a defeatist attitude and weak will cannot take the strain. Most of the pilgrims return to Darchen from Drira-punkh after having darshan of the North face of Kailash. However it is believed that spiritual merit from the parikrama can be gained only if the entire parikrama is completed. By abandoning the parikrama mid way one loses the merit gained so far. There is no such thing as part merit from part parikrama.

Kailash Mansarovar region has remained a sacred place for people of many faiths for the past thousands of years. But surprisingly there is not a single temple or an enshrined statue or Photograph of any God in this region. In the ancient times this region was a part of the kingdom of Hindu kings. Most Hindu kings patronized arts and science and encouraged construction of massive temples and places of worship as it was one of the means to fulfill the duty of providing welfare to the people.

But surprisingly, even the Hindu kings of the bygone era never attempted to build any temple in this region. Perhaps this region itself is a temple. The rivers Karnali, Brahmaputra, Indus and Sutlej have their origin in this region. In terms of quantity of water, Karnali is the largest tributary of the Ganga. It is also the longest tributary of the Ganga. Karnali originates from Mansarovar, flows through the eastern part of Nepal and then cuts across the Sivalik mountain ranges and flows through Uttar Pradesh to merge with the Ganga in Bihar. Karnali is a major tourist attraction in Nepal, as it is ideally suited for river rafting. Tourists are also attracted by the Dolphins found in Karnali. The Brahmaputra flows in southern part of Tibet, before it enters India in Arunachal Pradesh. Thereafter it flows through Assam and Bangladesh, before it empties itself into the Bay of Bengal. The Sutlej flows westward through Himachal Pradesh, Punjab, Sind before finally meeting the Arabian Sea near the port city of Karachi. The Indus flows through Ladakh in India and then enters Pakistan. In ancient India, river Indus was known as the river Sindhu. The Greeks called the river Sindu as Indica and called the people of Bharat as the people of river Indica. Through the ages, many great civilizations have developed and flourished on the banks of these great rivers

In Drira Phuk we stayed at a guest house which is built on a low lying, very large sized flat stone and has large rooms arranged in a square. Each room accommodates about 15 pilgrims. There are no bathrooms or toilets. Perhaps this is the only building in this area. Kailash is about 800 meters away from this place. From the guest house one can have the darshan of the North face of Kailash. During sun rise and sun set the Kailash turns bright golden.

We reached Drira Phuk in the evening. It is biting cold and the temperature is much below zero degree. After having tea and chatting with other pilgrims, I thought of doing some asanas and pranayams and so I took a blanket and went to a nearby hillock. There was a big Tibetan dog sitting some distance away from where I laid the blanket. It was curiously looking at me, but when it saw me lying down and stretching on the blanket, the dog also lowered its head, relaxed and came in the sleeping position as if it was saying – feel at ease man, I will not bother you. I could not do much asanas as it started snowing. By the time I returned to the guest house I was wet. In this area, perhaps due to the high altitude and the cold temperature, it never rains, there is only snowfall. One elderly pilgrim scolded me by saying that he did not know that I so foolish that I would go out in the snow instead of meditating and resting in the room. Some of us wanted to go to the foot of Kailash, but we were told that besides paucity of time, the area immediately surrounding Kailash has high velocity winds and it is not safe to go there as many times the pilgrims just disappear from there without a trace. Someone told me that there is also an inner parikrama(circumambulation) of Kailash, done during the Hindu calendar month of 'Shravan' by some highly spiritually developed persons. I'am not sure if it is true. Mountaineering or climbing on Kailash is perhaps prohibited even by the Chinese Government. Kailash is worshipped as the abode of Shivji or perhaps Shivji himself. Kailash can be conquered only by love and devotion. In the late evening I sat on a bench watching Kailash. After some time I could see a face like formation having two eyes and two eyebrows and a line which looked like a nose on the Kailash. I showed it to another pilgrim, who at the first glance could not see it but after a few seconds said that "yes I can also see two smiling mysterious eyes as if they were looking at us". I took a photograph of Kailash. In the photograph one can see the two eyes, if seen carefully by enlarging the photograph. It is believed that one parikrama of Kailash can wash away the defilements of many lives. 108 parikramas can raise a person to Buddhahood.

(North face of Kaiash. Turns Golden at sun set and sun rise)

At sunset, at about 9.45 p.m., Kailash became shining golden yellow. After taking a few more photographs, I retired to my bed and as per the practice followed by me for the past few days, I started writing the diary of the happenings and experiences during the day. While I'am writing this diary, a lady sleeping on a bed adjacent to my bed has started vomiting. This woke up the other pilgrims, who brought water and asked for the doctor. The lady was shouting and complaining that there was no one to attend to her although she had paid a high fee for the Yatra(pilgrimage). After some time, the Sherpa leader-Rampal came to our room, with some Khicchdi and started persuading the sick lady to eat the Khiccdi. But the lady was adamant and she refused to open her mouth. It was perhaps due to the stress caused by the 'Yatra' at high altitude. The Sherpa was saying; "madamji, if you do not eat how will you get well". Two sherpas caught the lady and held her down while the Sherpa leader put food and then water in her month, which she finally swallowed. This made me realize that even I had hardly consumed any water during the past 12 hours. I immediately reached for the bottle but found that it was empty. I thought of asking the Sherpas to get me some drinking water, but I restrained myself as they were busy helping the sick. After the Sherpas left, I went outside the room to search for water, but the barrels kept outside were empty. Before retiring I could not help taking one last look at Kailash. The guest house had gone to sleep and the lights were switched off. But in the quietness of the whistling winds Kailash looked awake, as if it was watching the sleepy dark night. The sky over Kailash is lit up with numerous constellations of stars, with one bright most conspicuous star exactly above Kailash.

9

THE SECOND DAY OF THE CIRCUMAMBULATION OF KAILASH

Date-5th June

I did not get good sleep last night and when I woke up in the morning I was having a headache and I was feeling weak and tired and feverish. I had to pull myself out of the bed. This sudden deterioration in my health made me feel worried and sad. Today's parikrama(circumambulation) was the most difficult one as it required climbing for 8 kms to a height of 18,600 feet on the Drolma Pass and walking a total distance of 28 Kms to reach a place called Zutrul Phuk, before sun set. Thanks to my reading and interest in knowing about the difficulties one faces at high altitude, I could immediately make a guess that I was suffering from dehydration as the symptoms were of dehydration. I had forgotten to drink water the previous day. In cold climate one does not feel as thirsty as in the plains, but none the less one should keep on drinking water, at least 8 liters per day. Drinking water and smelling the Kapur (camphor) are the two cardinal rules while Trekking at high altitude. Water keeps the body hydrated and the kapur keeps the air passage clean. Today we were to walk the distance of 28 kms and so I did not have much time. I immediately went outside and drank a few glasses of water. I took my stick and started walking with the others. Out of the many pilgrims who had come with us from Yam Dwar to Dera Punkh, only about 10 of us are to do the parikrama(circumambulation) of the second day. The rest of the pilgrims went back to Darchen. Some who had come on horse- back had more time, started some time after us. But even those on horse- back have to walk and climb some distance on reaching the base of Drolma Pass.

(pilgrims on the second day of parikrama of Kailash)

Despite drinking many glasses of water before embarking on the second day of parikrama, my tiredness was not going away. I could walk only a few steps, before stopping, as my head was aching and I was feeling exhausted and weak. Just yesterday I was robust and almost ran through the distance of 15 kms and today I could barely take a few steps without stopping to catch my breath. Adding to my woes was my companion Bhupatsingh. Every now and then he stopped, looked back at me and said "bana walk fast or go back to the camp, the other pilgrims have gone much ahead of us." For the first time in my life I found myself in such an embarrassing and frustrating situation. My mind was keen and interested in seeing the Drolma Pass, the river Indus and what lay ahead, but my body was not cooperating. Bhupatsingh looked hale and hearty and was walking with his head held high as if he was a soldier on a mission to complete the padyatra. His will–power and determination were commendable. We are both from a place called Deodar in Gujarat. We had come together and are suppose to remain together. Many thoughts crossed my mind– "maybe I was a sinner and therefore I was feeling exhausted", "I may have caught a cold or flu as I had become wet in the snow fall yesterday evening", "so what if I cannot walk fast, I'am at least able to walk", "Bhupatsingh is a teetotaler, whereas I gulp down many cups of tea during the day. I should restrict tea intake to two cups a day" "it is only dehydration and I will get well soon" and many other thoughts clouded by mind. Taking long walks is a delight and a favorite pastime for many. Even the most indolent enjoys a leisurely walk in the lap of nature. But here walk is not a leisurely activity, but it is hard work. This is truly the mother of all walks. After some time I was joined by a lady pilgrim, who looked even more tired and exhausted than myself. Later I came to know that her name was Ritaben and she was from Rajkot. She had come for the yatra for the second time. During the first time, which was a year before, she was afflicted by mountain sickness when she reached Mansarovar and she had to be immediately evacuated to Nepal. I was told that even when she was on a stretcher, she was saying that if she dies her mortal remains should be left in the river Brahmaputra. She told me with great difficulty that she is finding it extremely difficult to walk. I said that she should repeat the Shiv mantra-"Om Namah Shivay" twenty times and take one step for every mantra and then stop and repeat Shiv Mantra ten times before again walking 20 steps. She said I was a great support to her. A strange thought crossed my mind-'What if I die here?' 'will I be reborn in Tibet?' Almost all religions of the world believe in the doctrine of reincarnation. All who are born have to die and all that dies is reborn. When a person dies only his Karma- merit and demerit survives. Nothing of the individual survives. Knowledge, memory, relationships, wealth are lost forever. Only the tendencies remain. As the Buddhist saying- 'From all that he loves, man must part'.

After walking about two hours, and slowly sipping two bottles of water, my condition started improving and I started feeling more warm and energetic. But Ritaben looked the same. If one sits down then the requirement of oxygen by the body decreases and one feels normal. But due to the time constrains one cannot rest for long as the thought that one would be left behind and the sun will set is a constant botheration. Bhupatsingh had not gone far as every now and then he was stopping to see how I was faring. Perhaps he considers it his duty and responsibility to look after me. Now that I had started feeling better, I picked up speed and caught up with Bhupatsingh. The enthusiasm and interest that had left me today morning was returning. I told Bhupatsing that the lady Ritaben is in her middle age and she appears to be unwell and that we cannot leave her. Bhupatsing looked very tense and serious and was perhaps not enjoying the walk. He frowned and said; "if she is to die, she will die what we can do about it". Harsh words! But perhaps what he wanted to say was that it was beyond our powers, as we were only instruments in the hands of fate. I somehow could not leave her to her fate and every now and then I slowed down to walk with her. Despite the suffocation and her eyes bulging out, I found that she was determined to continue and finish the yatra. After some time we were joined by two Shearpas, who were carrying oxygen cylinders on their backs. This greatly relieved me as there was someone to look after the lady.

Initially when we left the camp at Drira Punkh, we could see Kailash on our right side. But after walking some distance, the Kailash was not visible. We came across snow covered areas on our way, but the snow was as hard as rock and we could easily walk over it. After some time we were joined by another group of three persons who had left earlier and were ahead of us, but had now slowed down due to fatigue. We were walking some distance —about 10 meters- and then stopping and taking rest on a way side rock. I found that the pilgrims were not enjoying walking and were trying to give a sense of purpose to the parikrama(circumambulation). One of the pilgrim said that the demon king Ravana had done penance at this place, which made him a powerful and a wealthy king. Another asked what Ravana had achieved after a 1000 years of penance. After a few years of rule over Lanka, he was defeated by Lord Rama. The three pilgrims who had joined us also looked tired, bewildered and disillusioned. Ritaben, who was now behind us was suffering. Bhupatsingh looked tense and angry. The two sherpas accompanying Ritaben looked bogged down by the weight of the rucksack and Oxygen cylinders on their backs. I was much better than what I was today morning and my stamina had improved, but I still had a headache and I was feeling somewhat tired and low. I started wondering as to why we were not enjoying the padyatra(circumambulation on foot). After-all we had come to the home of our heavenly father to enjoy and experience divinity and not to suffer. I asked one of the pilgrims if he knew the Mrityunjay mantra. He said yes and he recited the mantra: **"Om tryambhakam yajamahe sugandhim pushtivardhanam; urvarukamiva bandhanam, mrityor mukshiya maamrital"** Which when translated to English means- "O praise to the three eyed One, who increases prosperity, who has a sweet fragrance, who frees the world from all diseases and death! Liberate- as the ripe fruit from the wine. Shiva grant immortality." Just then four horsemen crossed us. Seeing us the horsemen stopped and came to me. I could not understand what they were saying, but I could make out that they were willing to give me a horse on hire. I pointed at a young white horse meaning thereby that I would like to hire that horse. But one of the horseman started shaking his head quite intensely, with eyes closed, in disapproval and he took off his hat and started tossing some pieces of paper kept inside the hat. I picked up one piece of paper from the hat and gave it to the horseman. The horseman saw the piece of paper and straightened the reins of one of the horses, indicating thereby that I was to ride that horse. I asked Bhupatsing if he would like to ride a horse. He appeared hesitant and then he said "no, you ride". The base of the Drolma Pass was 6 kms from where we were. I paid the horseman 60 yens and he agreed to give me the horse till the base of the Drolma Pass. I mounted the horse and gave a slight kick and pulled the reins and the horse went into a full gallop. This greatly pleased the other horsemen. They were laughing and they came galloping on their horses by my side. I came across a herd of Yaks' going on the road in front of me. I signaled the horse to go down the road and the slope of the hillock so as to overtake the yaks, and the horse immediately went down the slope of the hillock, galloped and after crossing the herd of yaks again climbed the hillock, and I was again on the road with the herd of Yaks now behind me. I thoroughly enjoyed riding this Tibetan horse. Tibetan horses are much smaller in size then the Marwari breed of horses. But they are said to be very strong and of good temperament. The

Moghul Invaders- Chengiz Khan, Timur the lame and Babur are said to have come to India on these breed of horses.

After reaching the base of Drolma pass, I saw that the climb was not very steep. So I took the horse some distance on the slope of the Drolma pass. But the slope was covered by snow, and the horseman, who was behind me asked me to dismount. I realized that the horse may slip on the snowy slope and cause injury to it and also to me. This horse was really a spirited one and it would have climbed the Drolma Pass with me on its back, had I not dismounted. After climbing for some distance, the slope became almost vertical at about 70 degrees. I was using the stick and one hand to support myself and climb. One has to go on poking the stick in the snow in front to make sure that the snow does not give way when you step on it. I found climbing the vertical slope really exhausting. I was feeling breathless and suffocated as if there was no air to breath. A few steps left me heaving for breath. At one point I felt as if my lungs had stopped working. But pausing for some time and resting the torso on the rocks brings one back to normalcy. This climb has claimed many lives in the past. I was told that yesterday a lady who was trying to climb while riding a Yak fell into the frozen Drolma pass river and died. Many just collapse here. The Hindu dead are flow back to India. Those belonging to other religions leave the body of the dead in the slopes and river adjoining the Drolma pass. But despite the fatigue I was going through, not once did I fell that I would die. I could feel my brain and lungs craving for oxygen and my heart working hard. But my legs felt strong and I did not have the slightest of doubt that my body may collapse. Taking firm small steps, one at a time, fixing my gaze on the grey snowy surface of the rocks, I kept moving my feet forward. Many people, especially Tibetan pilgrims easily climb the Drolma Pass while doing Kora. Perhaps I had not done enough exercise to build up my stamina for the Parikrama. Exercise increases the capacity of the lungs by increasing the number of the oxygen carrying capillaries. I realized that had I done jogging with a ruck-sack full of stones on my back for a month before coming to Kailash, I would have been saved from the exhaustion which I went through while climbing the Drolma Pass. When I reached the top of the Drolma Pass I came to a flat open place covered at many places with cloth pieces having the Buddhist mantra written on them and tied in a rope. It was about 2 p.m and the Drolma Pass appeared like a bazzar with many Buddhists and Sherpas and Yaks crowding the flat surface. I had no idea which route was taken by these people to reach the top of Drolma pass. But it seems there are many pathways leading to the flat surface. After reaching the top flat plane of Drolma Pass, I was feeling fresh and healthy and my headache and fatigue were completely gone.

I saw an elderly Buddhist Monk seated on a large rock at the Drolma Pass. I wished him good afternoon and sat near him on an adjoining rock. I asked him if he could understand English. He smiled and said yes. Seeing that he was smiling and interested in talking I asked him "Sir what is the essence of Buddhism." He again smiled and said: "it is practice. Sit at one place and concentrate on your breath and you will come to know yourself." This reminded me of the famous saying of Buddha that one who has lived for only 30 years but has learnt to witness the rising the passing and the waning (of emotions and desires) has lived more than one who lives for 100 years without learning to witness the same. He further said that "if you want worldly possessions and success then you have to toil, sweat, strive and achieve.

But that will only make a difference externally. Internally you will be the same or you may become even worse. Then I asked him "Sir what is the difference between a worldly man and a spiritual man or a monk." He said: "Subconscious mind of a worldly man is filled with many unfulfilled desires, anxiety of the future, regrets of the past, anger, sorrow, grief, inferiority and superiority complex, attachment to objects and aversions and impressions of strained relationships and when he dies he dies with all this burden of unfulfilled desired and regrets. Whereas a God man transcends his body, mind and intellect and is therefore free, happy and immortal." After talking to this monk, I felt truly blessed and I resolved that when I die I would die completely free from all desires, regrets and sorrow. I was told that there are a number of caves hidden in the mountains from where the path of the parikrama passes. Many great saints have meditated in these caves. But unfortunately we were racing with time and were so obsessed with coping with the fatigue and breathlessness that we did not have the will to visit these caves. The most widely used pilgrim guide to Kailash was written by a Kagyu monk about a century ago. His guide book is based on oral traditions and ancient texts. It is impossible for a pilgrim to visit even half the sites given in this book.

The snow covered surface of the Drolma Pass, at an altitude of 18,600 feet, refreshes the memories of the Yeti -- the abominable Snowman of Tibet. Yeti has always been a subject of fascination for the young and the old. As a child I was a fan of Tintin-the hero in the Tintin series of books for children. I still have a faint memory of the encounter of Tintin with a Yeti in the book titled 'Tintin in Tibet'. For the local Tibetans, Yeti is a part of Tibetan culture and mythology. In 1953, during the expedition which scaled the Mount Everest and reached the summit for the very first time, the mountaineers Hillary and Tanzen reported to have seen foot marks of Yeti on the Mount Everest at an altitude of 20,000/- feet. There are recorded instances when mountaineers have seen a large creature on two legs walking on the snowy slopes of the Himalayan Mountains. It could not be followed due to the sheer speed with which it moved and vanished in the snowy peaks. But on examining the place where it was spotted, large size foot prints were found. Such foot prints have been photographed, samples taken and preserved. A Yeti's footprint in snow is about 7 inches longer and four inches wider than that of a full grown human. According to folklore in Nepal, there used to be a whole village inhabited by Yetis on the slopes of Mount Everest. But one day in a drinking feast organized in the village, the inebriated Yetis fought among themselves and killed each other. Only one family which had not participated in the feast survived. But being vulnerable after the destruction of the village, the family migrated to the upper region of Mount Everest. The Himalayan region has high mountains with dense vegetation and deep plunging valleys on the Indian side and high plateaus with inhospitable climate on the Chinese side. It is impossible for any scientific expedition to survey these areas to ascertain the whereabouts of a Yeti. The Tibetans say that the Yetis are mystical beings and can disappear in thin air at will.

Some believe that what the mountaineers see is not a Yeti but a human hermit.

The descent from the Drolma Pass is a gradual one stretching for about 2 kms before reaching the flat plane of river Indus at 17,000/- feet. Some distance from the flat surface of the Drolma Pass is the Gauri Kund. It is a small lake which was half covered with ice. The water of Gauri Kund is said to be very holy. It is not advisable for the pilgrims to go down the steep slope filled with rocks with sharp edges to fetch water of Gauri Kund. Sherpas charge 10 yens for fetching water of Gauri Kund. Today this entire area: the Drolma Pass, the narrow pathway going down from the Drolma Pass, was full of people and animals and it appeared like the C.G road of Ahmedabad. There were pilgrims, Buddhists Monks, Indian pilgrims, yaks carrying luggage and tribal people with the yaks. But the horsemen and their horses were missing. Perhaps they take the horses across the Drolma Pass from some other route. This area is well connected with mobile phone networks and most people with mongoloid features have mobile phones with them. Foreigners have to activate their mobile phone by buying some special activation cards in China. Others and I in my group were not using Mobile phones as we were not aware of such activation cards.

On the pathway which passes from the Gauri Kund, some Tibetan girls sit with bottles filled with Gauri Kund water. I had some dates and a Cadbury Chocolate, which I gave to a lady who was a porter and she in return gave me a bottle of Gauri Kund water, which I immediately drank. Most people take the

Gauri Kund water home as it is pure and holy. But I, having experienced the debilitating effect of dehydration, was gulping down as much water as I could. Gauri Kund means the Kund or pool of the Goddess. Goddess is the source of spiritual energy. By worshiping the Goddess, the spiritual energy increases. The various tendencies found in humans are broadly categorized as Tamsic, Rajasic and Satvik. Indolence, dullness, delusions, confusion, cruelty and the like are tamsic tendencies. Activity, desires, passions are rajasic tendencies and calmness, detachment, truthfulness, learning, health promoting habits and the like are Satvik tendencies. An average person has all the three types of tendencies in him. Spiritual energy helps a tamsic person to become rajasic and a rajasic person to become satvik. Only a person with purely satvik tendencies can know and reach Shiva. After knowing Shiva, even the satvik tendencies are thrown away and the person becomes 'nirguni' or without any tendencies. There is a sloka in the vedic poem called 'Hinglaj Struti' sung in praise of Goddess Hinglaj, which reads as follows: "**nikunj kam krodh daitya, asur-kal mardani. Namottutsa mata Hinglaj nirmala niranjani.**" Which means- "take out lust, anger, evil from me, O destroyer of demons. I bow to mother Hingalaj, the pure and the formless one." From the Drolma Pass there is a 1500 feet descent to the plains of river Indus.

(Gauri Kund)

While descending the slope of Drolma Pass, I met Parmarbhai Parmar, and one lady who introduced herself as a school teacher. Both of them have come from Gujarat. We sat on rocks by the path-way and chatted for some time. Later today evening I was told that this lady had suddenly collapsed while walking and she was taken on a stretcher by the sherpas. I could not believe it. When I met her on the slope with Parmarbhai she looked healthy and happy. The Sherpas equipped with mobile phones and the oxygen cylinders are doing commendable work and have saved many lives. Everything here looks almost the same. There is the sun, there is the earth, there is cool breeze, there are mountains and rivers, but the percentage of oxygen in the air is less and the body of a person who has come from the sea level does not easily acclimatize to the new altitude. This causes the hardship. At one place, while descending on the slope, I and Parmarbhai were waiting for the path-way to clear-up as there were some pilgrims descending on their hinges in front of us. Suddenly we saw a yak running down towards us from behind us on the path-way where we were standing. I had a fairly big size walking stick with a brass handle in my right hand. I pointed the stick towards the Yak and said "stop stop stop", and the Yak suddenly stopped as if it was an automobile and had applied brakes. We went on the side of the path and after sometime when the descending path-way was clear of pilgrims, I lowered the stick and the Yak again ran with the same ferocity. Some said my stick has acquired the power because it has done the parikrama (circumambulation) with me and so it could stop a yak gone berserk and running in a frenzy. Parmarbhai, who is in the police, said that the yak owners thrash the yaks and so the yaks are very obedient and afraid of human beings.

On descending from the slopes and on reaching the flat surface, there are stores and restaurants housed in tents. An energy drink-Red Bull- seems to be the favorite of the tourists, pilgrims and Tibetans as it is easily available and very common here. I was told by a Sherpa that one should not drink more than one bottle of Red Bull per day as it has very high calorie content. The only people we can talk to are Sherpas who come from Nepal with the pilgrims. Tibetan and Chinese do not understand our language. One peculiar thing about the Tibetans and the local people here is that irrespective of their age or gender or the type of clothes they wear–whether traditional or modern–, all of them have a 'mala' of beads around their necks. Whenever they get time they take the 'mala' in their hand and they start reciting the mantra.

I sat on a rock near a shop-tent and waited for Bhupatsingh. After about half an hour Bhupatsingh emerged from the slopes and came towards me. He was slightly limping. He said his shoe was hurting his toe. We both had some snacks and a bottle of Red Bull each. Thereafter, we again started walking. The remaining journey of about 12 kms to reach Zutraa Phukh looked very easy. The difficult part of the parikrama was over and we felt relaxed and at ease. The Tibetan porter who had given me a bottle of Gauri Kund water came to us and said something which we could not understand. She extended her arm towards me and started walking fast. At first I could not understand, but then I thought that perhaps she wanted us to walk with her. We started walking with her at her speed. She was walking quite fast and initially it was difficult to stay abreast. Bhupatsingh lagged behind as his shoe was hurting him. Initially increasing the walking speed so as to walk with the porter girl caused breathlessness. But surprisingly after some time I started enjoying the fast walk. A Tibetan boy also joined us. The three of us held each other's hands and walked very fast shoulder to shoulder and we left the other pilgrims far behind us. In the last two days of walking this was the first time when I enjoyed walking. Otherwise, walking here is more of a burden then an activity in spiritual pursuit. We reached Zutra Phunk in the evening before sun set. We are lodged in small rooms made from tin sheets. Each room accommodates three persons.

Yak carrying luggage

10

THE THIRD DAY OF THE CIRCUMAMBULATION OF KAILASH

Date 6th June, 2013

I got up early, feeling refreshed and energetic. In the Kailash Mansarovar region there are no insects or reptiles. The air is free from mosquitoes and other insects commonly found at sea level. I' am told that there are no snakes or crocodiles in the lakes or rivers in this region. But Tibetan dogs called bontias are a common sight. I went to the bank of river Indus which is about 500 meters from the camp. While returning, four large size Tibetan dogs came barking at me from four different directions. But their barks sounded as if they were playing. One can make out from the sound of the barks, when a dog is furious and when it is trying to play. I was not afraid and I raised both my hands and shouted, and the dogs immediately dispersed. A street dog will usually not allow a stranger to go away so easily. But, strangely, these dogs did not try to follow me nor did they howl at me once I shouted and raised my hands. When I tilted by head to see if a dog was following me, I saw a large size dog stretching its neck and pointing its nose towards me as if it was trying to smell me.

(River Indus)

The 12 kms walk from Zutra Phuk to Darchen is by the side of river Indus and is very pleasant and enjoyable. At one place we came across stones which had impressions of a cows hoofs and a man's foot on them. These stones are worshiped by the Buddhist, the Hindus and the Jains. It is believed that Shivji and his mount Nandi usually stay in light form. But at this particular place, they had descended on earth in their physical bodies, which made these impressions on the stone

When we reached Darchen, the pilgrims who did not come for the parikrama of Kailash and those who had returned to Darchen from Drira Phuk were waiting to receive us. They were very glad to see us and the young pilgrims touched our feet and the elderly pilgrims embraced us. The pilgrims who did the parikrama had a story to tell, whereas the pilgrims who stayed back were only curious to know how it was and what happened.

From Darchen we went to Mansarovar Lake by road. Thus in the last three days we have done the parikrama (circumambulation) of 80 kms around Mansarovar lake by road and the padyatra (circumambulation on foot) of 58 kms around Kailash. When we reached Mansarovar in the afternoon, it was warm, sunny and pleasant. We took a bath in the Mansarovar. Unlike the previous time, which was on the 2nd of June, today the water was not so cold and the pilgrims really enjoyed taking dips in the holy water. I took 40 dips in the water. I had thought of swimming in the lake, but somehow I completely forgot about swimming once I entered the lake and I only took dips and kept counting them.

11

THE 'DARSHAN' OF MYSTERIOUS LIGHTS AT MANSAROVAR

Date 7ᵗʰ June, 2013

At about 4 a.m Shamlal woke me up and said that he had gone to the Lake and had darshan of a light which was floating and dancing over the lake. Seeing lights coming from the sky and then disappearing is not uncommon at the Mansarovar lake. Many pilgrims in the past have reported having seen such lights. It is believed that at dawn, 'Devis' and 'Devtas' come for taking a bath in the lake and give darshan to pilgrims present near the lake. I tried to wake up Bhupatsingh, but he was in deep slumber and did not wake up. There was no one in the room willing to accompany me to the lake side. Some ladies sat by the side of the window facing the lake. But the lake is 200 meters away from the tin tents where we are staying and therefore in the dark one cannot see the lake from the room window. I decided to go to the lake alone. I took the torch and went outside. Outside the tents, I met a lady who said that she was in room no.4 and was unable to locate her room and if I can help her to find room no.4. While I was taking her to room no. 4 I met Vijaybhai, who is a

Brahmin from Rajkot and knows many slokhs and hymns from the ancient Hindu scriptures. Vijaybhai was accompanied by a lady. In the dark I could recognize Vijaybhai from his voice, but I have no idea who the two ladies were. Vijaybhai and the lady said that they were going to the lake. The lady of room no. 4 said that she would also like to accompany us to the lake. So the four of us went to the lake and sat in the sand near the lake. This time I had not taken the mala with me and I did not recite the mantras. I enjoyed feeling the environment by the lake side at dawn: the purity and calmness by the side of the lake, the pure cool air caressing my face, the musical sound of water moving in the lake, the dark sky with twinkling stars, the soft sand and pebbles underneath. Vijaybhai was singing some Sanskrit prayers in his sweet melodious voice. After about half an hour I looked towards my right towards Kailash and I saw about seven stars like lights arranged in the form of a Shivling in the sky. I showed the lights to Vijaybhai. After a few seconds the lights disappeared and then again reappeared to our extreme right. We got up and repositioned ourselves so that we faced the lights. The lights again disappeared and one star like light started moving slowly towards us. Then suddenly the light made two quick movements towards us and I felt as if the light would be upon us with one more such fast move or stride. I could somehow feel the love and confidence emanating from the light as if it were some great warrior-saint advancing towards us in the open plain before us. Initially for a second or so, when the light took rapid strides towards us, I felt uneasy and somewhat nervous, but then I felt completely captivated or hypnotized by the light and for a few seconds I felt as if there was nothing else around me except the light in the front. This memory of the light suddenly moving fast towards us and filling the space in the front of us is the strongest in my mind, as if it has got deeply ingrained in my mind. Then the light stopped and started moving slowly, parallel to us, and then disappeared. This must have lasted for a few minutes. I had joined my hands in a 'namaste' and I was reciting the Shiv Mantra. Vijaybhai said that a 'Devta' had given us 'darshan'. I started wondering whether it could be a UFO (unidentified flying object) or some advanced machine which can move is such a way and react to our thoughts and emotions. When we were returning to the camp, Vijaybhai said that we cannot see air, but air is there in the same way we cannot see God but God is there. The ancient Hindu scriptures say that an accomplished yogi can turn his body into light form or can disappear altogether. Perhaps what we saw was an accomplished yogi who gave us 'darshan'. In this region of Kailash-Mansarovar, many pilgrims have experiences, which do not have a rational scientific explanation. This mystical experience of the occult strengthens one's faith in the supernatural. One is compelled by reason to accept that there is something more than the mundane world. There is a state of existence which is different and higher than what we are aware of.

We left Mansarovar at about 8 a.m. for Sangha in Land Rover jeeps. We had spent two days at Mansarovar. One was on the 2nd before the parikrama of Kailash and the second was today i.e. 7th June after the parikrama of Kailash. I felt that our stay at Mansarovar was a very short one. There is a lot to learn and experience in this region. This is truly the abode of the Gods. This region is preferred by yogis and saints for penance and deep meditation as the environment here is pure and charged with the spiritual energy. Besides experiencing the occult, a pilgrim can also enjoy his stay here if he looks after his health and is well equipped to deal with the harsh unpredictable weather conditions. According to me, the bare minimum a pilgrim should carry with him on this pilgrimage is as under:

1. Medicines: Dimox tablets (take after an altitude of 8,000/- feet), Camphor (kapur), brufane or combiflam, cold and cough medicine, other medicines according to the specific aliments or body condition of the pilgrim.

2. Warm Clothes: pair of thermal(inner) wear, woolen sweater, woolen monkey cap, woolen hand-gloves and woolen socks, down-jacket (down-jacket is usually supplied by the tour operator), rain coat, goggles, sun screen lotion, water-proof trekking shoes.

3. Other items: Toilet paper, torch, insulated water bottle. Devotion to God, willingness to help those in need and a quiet and serene mind.

We reached Sangha at about 7 p.m in the evening. We were put up in a hotel which has modern westernized rooms with attached bathrooms. Later today, one pilgrim told of a strange dream he had the previous night at the Mansarovar lake. In his dream he saw himself strolling with two of his friends near the lake. Suddenly a demon appeared from behind him and he felt as if the demon wanted to devour him. Being frightened he started running to save himself and the demon started chasing him. While trying to hide and escape from the demon he saw a big palace and he decided to hide inside the palace. When he entered the palace, he came across a big hall where some ladies were dancing. From among the many ladies, one extremely beautiful lady dressed in traditional Indian clothes noticed him and came towards him and touched his hand. As soon as she touched him he experienced a sexual orgasm. Strange as it may sound, but many people have reported to have had extreme wet-dreams at the Mansarovar lake.

12

RETURNING TO NEPAL

Date 8th June, 2013

We started from Shangah in the morning and reached the China border in the afternoon. We went through the usual checking at the China border. Chinese authorities are very strict and pilgrims are not allowed to take water–even the holy water of Mansarovar – or plants or shrubs across the border. Pilgrims who had taken large cans of the Mansarovar water had to leave the cans at the border check post. I had taken the Mansarovar water in two 1 liter bottles. The bottles were kept in-between the clothes and went unnoticed at the border check post. At the border there are agents who exchange yens (Chinese currency) with the Nepali rupees. We had lunch after entering Nepal. There are many shops and restaurants on both sides of the border between China and Nepal. We went to the Gokarna Forest Resort and rested in the luxurious rooms of the Resort.

13

THE CITY OF KHATMANDU AND THE MYSTICAL RUDRAKHS BEADS

Date-9ᵗʰ June, 2013

For the last ten years Nepal is undergoing a transition from a monarchy to a democracy. Monarchy was overthrown by a populist uprising against the king. However, we are told that the constitution is still in the process of being enacted. It is not certain whether Nepal is a Hindu state or a secular state.

Today, in the morning we went to the Pashupati Nath Temple. It is a Shiv temple. Pundits charge Rs. 1,000/- for the Rudra-abheshek Puja. I gave Rs. 1,000/- to a pundit, who promised to do a Rudra-abhishek Puja the next day. He asked for my name and my surname and the name of the saint who is my 'gotra'. This, he said, was my unique identity. Using this identity he promised to do the 'Rudraabhishek puja' in my name, the next morning.

Inside the premises of the temple is the Samadhi of the saint Sankaracharya. Sankaracharya, one of the most revered saints of India, passed away at a young age of 29 years. But during this short life span, he revived Hinduism in India and established four

'Matths' in the four corners of India. 'Matths' – centers for leaning and practicing Hinduism– were of great significance in ancient India. The Belur Matth established by Swami Vivekanand is even today a well know centre for learning and spiritualism. Most 'Matths' provided free food to poor and disseminate information on health and spiritualism. They also provide basic amenities to those who have renounced the world to practice Yoga. 'Matths' have their own income and they hold land and property given away in donations.

(Pashupatinath temple at Kathmandu in Nepal)

Outside the temple there are many shops selling Rudraks beads. Rudraks beads are obtained from Rudraks plant. Beads grow on the Rudraksh plants as lemons grow on a lemon tree. Rudrakhs beads are used for enhancing health and positive energy. A person wearing Rudraks beads is protected from negativity. They act as a shield against negative forces. Ancient scriptures lay great emphasis on the Rudraksh beads for spiritual purposes. They help a worldly person to fulfill his worldly desires and also attain Moksha. They are mood elevators and improve concentration. Wearing these beads and drinking water obtained after soaking beads overnight in it cures high blood pressure.

A Rudraks bead has deep seated lines or groove on its surface. This line or groove is called 'mukh' or face of Rudrakhs. The number of such lines can vary from one to fourteen. If a bead is broken open, the number of compartments inside it is the same as the number of such lines or groove on its surface. Depending on the number of 'Mukhs', different beads have different effects: wearing one 'Mukhi' Rudraks helps a spiritual practitioner to experience deep meditation, a seven 'Mukhi' bead helps in gaining wealth, etc. A good quality bead is round in shape without any broken surface. They are found in three different sizes: the biggest ones are of the size of a lemon. The second variety is of the size of a blueberry. The smallest ones are of the size of chickpeas. The beads of the size of a lemon are rare. Even those in commercial production of Rudraks beads in large farms are not able to produce one 'Mukhi' Rudraks beads and beads of the size of a lemon. Beads have a see through hole at the centre and so they are woven into a thread and used for reciting mantras. They are available in four different colors- white, red, yellow and black. White Rudraksh enhances the powers of a person engaged in intellectual pursuits. Red Rudraks benefits those who guard the honor and security of the society. Yellow Rudrakhs helps in business. Black colored Rudraks should be worn by people who keep the society free from dirt and filth. When a good quality bead is kept between two copper coins it rotates.